INTRODUCTION

The focus of *Fourth-Grade Math Minutes* is math fluency—teaching students to solve problems effortlessly and rapidly. The problems in this book provide students with practice in key areas of fourth-grade math instruction, including

- fractions
- time
- angles
- story problems
- graphs
- long division
- plane and space figures
- multiplication
- standard and metric measurement
- perimeter, area, and volume
- addition and subtraction of decimals

Use this comprehensive resource to improve your students' overall math fluency, which will promote greater self-confidence in their math skills as well as provide the everyday practice necessary to succeed in a testing situation.

Fourth-Grade Math Minutes features 100 "Minutes." Each Minute consists of ten classroom-tested problems for students to complete in one minute. Each Minute includes questions of varying degrees of difficulty, integrating problem-solving and basic math skills. This unique format offers students an ongoing opportunity to improve their own fluency in a manageable, nonthreatening format. The quick, one-minute format combined with instant feedback makes this a challenging and motivational assignment students will look forward to each day. Students become active learners as they discover mathematical relationships and apply acquired understanding to the solution of realistic problems in each Minute.

How to Use This Book

Fourth-Grade Math Minutes is designed to be implemented in numerical order. Students who need the most support will find the order of skills as introduced most helpful in building and retaining confidence and success. For example, the first time that students are asked to compute the area of a shape, a possible answer is provided, and students must decide if the answer is true or false. Eventually, students are asked to compute the area without the support of a possible answer.

Fourth-Grade Math Minutes can be used in a variety of ways. Use one Minute a day for warm-up activities, bell-work, review, assessment, or a home-work assignment. Keep in mind that students will get the most benefit from their daily Minute if they receive immediate feedback. If you assign the Minute as homework, correct it in class at the beginning of the day.

If you use the Minutes as a timed activity, place the paper facedown on the students' desks, or display it as a transparency. Use a clock or kitchen timer to measure one minute. Encourage students to concentrate on completing each problem successfully and not to dwell on problems they cannot complete. At the end of the minute, have students stop working. Then, read the answers from the answer key (pages 108–112), or display them on a transparency. Have students correct their own work and record their score on the Minute Journal reproducible (page 6). Then, have the class go over each problem together to discuss the solution(s). Spend more time on problems that were clearly challenging for most of the class. Tell students that difficult problems will appear on future Minutes and they will have other opportunities for success.

Teach students strategies for improving their scores, especially if you time their work on each Minute. Tell students to

- leave more time-consuming problems for last
- come back to problems they are unsure of after they have completed all other problems
- make educated guesses when they encounter problems they are unfamiliar with
- rewrite word problems as number problems
- use mental math wherever possible

Students will learn to apply these strategies to other timed-test situations.

The Minutes are designed to improve math fluency and should not be included as part of a student's overall math grade. However, the Minutes provide an excellent opportunity for you to see which skills the class as a whole needs to practice or review. This knowledge will help you plan the content of future math lessons. A class that consistently has difficulty with reading graphs, for example, may make excellent use of your lesson in that area, especially if they know they will have other opportunities to achieve success in this area on future Minutes. Have students file their Math Journal and Minutes for that week in a location accessible to you both. Class discussions of the problems will help you identify which math skills to review. However, you may find it useful to review the Minutes on a weekly basis before sending them home with students at the end of the week.

While you will not include student Minute scores in your formal grading, you may wish to recognize improvements by awarding additional privileges or offering a reward if the entire class scores above a certain level for a week or more. Showing students that you recognize their efforts provides additional motivation to succeed!

Minute Journal

· ·

Name _____

MINUTE	DATE	SCORE	MINUTE	DATE	SCORE	MINUTE	DATE	SCORE	MINUTE	DATE	SCORE
1			26			51			76		
2			27			52			77		
3			28			53			78		
4			29			54			79		
5			30			55			80		
6			31			56			81		
7			32			57			82		
8			33			58			83		
9			34			59			84		
10			35			60			85		
11			36			61			86		
12			37			62			87		
13			38			63			88		
14			39			64			89		
15			40			65			90		
16			41			66			91		
17			42			67			92		
18			43			68			93		
19			44			69			94		
20			45			70			95		
21			46			71			96		
22			47			72			97		
23			48			73			98		
24			49			74			99		
25			50			75			100		

Fourth-Grade Math Minutes © 2002 Creative Teaching Press

SCOPE AND SEQUENCE

SKILL	MINUTE IN WHICH SKILL FIRST APPEARS
Congruency	1
Perimeter/Area/Volume	1
Expanded Form	1
Place Value	1
Addition	1
Story Problems	1
Subtraction	1
Money Calculations	1
Multiplication (up to multiples of 12)	1
Division (basic facts)	1
Patterning	2
Lines of Symmetry	2
Multiplication (one digit times two or more digits)	3
Greater Than/Less Than/Equal To	3
Fractions (calculation, equivalency, lowest terms)	4
Identifying Attributes of a Figure	6
Circle Graphs	6
Identifying and Comparing Fractions	7
Finding the Mean/Mode/Range	7
Money Equivalency	8
Time Equivalency	8
Even and Odd Numbers	9
Missing Elements in a Pattern	10
Rounding	10
Time Calculations	11
Angles	11
Standard Measurement (weight, length, distance, volume)	13
Metric Measurement (weight, length, distance, volume)	14
Identifying Angles	22
Decimals	24
Bar Graphs	26
Identifying Geometric Figures	32
Circles (radius, diameter)	38
Line Graphs	46
Ordered Pairs	51
Relating Fractions to Decimals	57
Relating Mixed Fractions to Decimals	60
Identifying Triangles	62
Improper Fraction to Mixed Number	70
Temperature (Fahrenheit and Celsius)	73

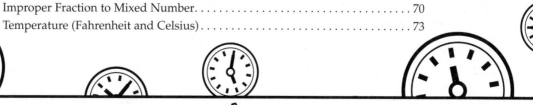

MINUTE 1

NAME _____

1. The area of the shape is 6 square units.
   Circle: True   or   False

2. Jenna wants to purchase a pad of drawing paper for $5.00, a charcoal pencil for $0.75, and an eraser for $1.25. How much money does she need altogether to buy the supplies? _____

3.   45
     + 4

4. Complete the fact family.
   5 x 7 = 35
   7 x 5 = _____
   35 ÷ 7 = _____
   35 ÷ 5 = _____

5. Circle the figure that matches the shaded figure:

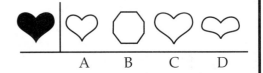

       A   B   C   D

6. The <u>difference</u> of 8 and 5 is _____.

7. The expanded form of 654 is 600 + 50 + _____.

8. The <u>sum</u> of 8 and 5 is _____.

For questions 9 and 10, circle the digit in the tens place.

9. 456

10. 925

Fourth-Grade Math Minutes © 2002 Creative Teaching Press

MINUTE 2

NAME _____

1. 15 − 8 =

2. 4, 8, 12, 16, 20, _____, _____, _____

3. 33
  + 5

4. Circle the figure that is congruent to the shaded figure:

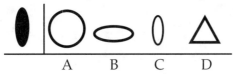

  A   B   C   D

5. 33
  − 5

6. Complete the fact family.
  6 x 7 = 42
  7 x 6 = _____
  42 ÷ 7 = _____
  42 ÷ 6 = _____

7. 12
  x 6

In questions 8–10, does the figure have a line of symmetry?
Write *yes* or *no*. If yes, draw a line of symmetry.

8.   _____

9.   _____

10.   _____

MINUTE 3

NAME _____

1. 4) 72

2. 21
   + 6

3. The volume of the shape is 9 cubic units.
Circle: True or False

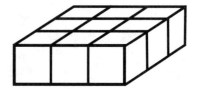

4. Complete the fact family.
5 x 8 = 40
8 x 5 = _____
40 ÷ 8 = _____
40 ÷ 5 = _____

5. Polly bought a new collar and leash for her dog. The total was $7.50.
She paid with a ten-dollar bill. How much change did she receive?
_____

6. 45
   − 3

7. 14
   x 5

Use <, >, or = to complete questions 8–10.

8. 3 _____ 13   **9.** 31 _____ 13   **10.** 310 _____ 310

Fourth-Grade Math Minutes © 2002 Creative Teaching Press

MINUTE 4

NAME _____

1. 85
      − 2

2. 7)35 (5) Which number is the <u>dividend</u> in this problem? _____

3. Riley has a 100-page book. She has read half of it. How many pages does she have left to read? _____ pages

4. Complete the fact family.
      9 x 4 = _____
      4 x 9 = _____
      36 ÷ 9 = _____
      36 ÷ 4 = _____

5. 4)28

6. 62
      + 7

7. 16
      x 7

For questions 8–10, write the equivalent fraction.

8. $\frac{2}{4}$ = _____

9. $\frac{3}{9}$ = _____

10. $\frac{2}{10}$ = _____

MINUTE 5

NAME _____

1. The area of the shape is 9 square units.
Circle: True   or   False

2. 3 x 5 = 15   Which number is the <u>product</u>? _____

3. 68
       – 5

4. Carol wants to buy 6 pens for $0.75 each. How much money does she need to buy the pens? _____

5. 21
       + 6

6. 8)72

7. The expanded form of 489 is 400 + _____ + 9.

8. 18
       x 6

For questions 9 and 10, write in the value of the underlined digit.

9. <u>5</u>0 = _____ tens

10. <u>7</u>0 = _____ tens

Fourth-Grade Math Minutes © 2002 Creative Teaching Press

MINUTE 6

NAME _____

1. 92
     + 3

2. 15
     x 8

3. The volume of the shape is 12 cubic units.
Circle: True   or   False

4. 6
     7)42   Which number is the <u>divisor</u>? _____

5. A quadrilateral has _____ sides and four angles.

6. 4)48

7. 54
     − 2

Use the circle graph to complete questions 8–10.

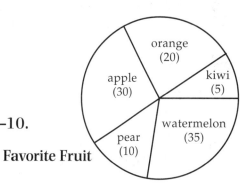

Favorite Fruit

8. How many people said pears are their favorite fruit? _____ people

9. Which fruit is the most popular? _____

10. The number of people who said apples are their favorite fruit equals
the sum of the number of people who said _____ and
_____ are their favorite fruit.

Fourth-Grade Math Minutes © 2002 Creative Teaching Press

MINUTE 7

NAME _____

1. Write the fraction that names the shaded portion. _____

2.
```
  29
-  7
```

3.
```
  54
+  4
```

4. What is the perimeter of the shape? _____

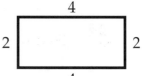

5. $6 \overline{)54}$

6. The expanded form of 3,024 is _____ + _____ + _____.

7.
```
  17
x  4
```

8. Identify the <u>mean</u> of the following numbers: 2, 4, 6. _____

For questions 9 and 10, circle the digit in the tens place.

9. 589

10. 546

Fourth-Grade Math Minutes © 2002 Creative Teaching Press

MINUTE 8

NAME _____

1. The area of the shape is 6 square inches.
Circle: True or False

3 in.

2 in.

2.   43
    + 7

3. 50 dimes = _____ dollars

4. 12 + 25 =

5.   19
      x 9

6. Sandy buys a box of chocolates. If the box costs $2.00 and there are
8 chocolates in the box, how much does each chocolate cost? _____

7.   84
    − 3

8. There are _____ minutes in 1 hour.

9. 78 x 100 =

10. 9)81

Fourth-Grade Math Minutes © 2002 Creative Teaching Press

MINUTE 9

NAME _____

1. Eleven is an odd number. Circle: True   or   False

2. 8)‾88‾

3. The volume of the shape is 21 cubic units.
   Circle: True   or   False

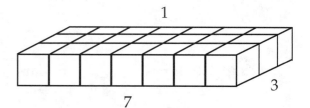

4.   37
   + 2
   ‾‾‾

5. A quadrilateral has _____ sides and _____ angles.

6.   57   7.   11
   – 6   x 6
   ‾‾‾   ‾‾‾

8. The expanded form of 103 is 100 + _____.

For questions 9 and 10, write +, –, or x to make the sentence true.

9.   17 – 4 _____ 10 = 23

10.   56 + 2 _____ 2 = 56

16

MINUTE 10

NAME _____

1.   13
     x 8

2.   84
         + 5

3. 2, 4, _____, 8, 10, 12

4. 30 ÷ 6 =

5.   58
       − 8

6. Identify the <u>range</u> of the following numbers: 2, 4, 8. _____

7. 6⟌36

For questions 8–10, round the number to the nearest ten. Circle the answer.

8. 156:   100   150   160   200

9. 78:   70   80   90   100

10. 52:   40   50   55   60

MINUTE 11

NAME _____

1. Identify the <u>mode</u> of the following numbers: 2, 4, 4, 5, 6. _____

2. Circle a reasonable measurement for the angle:
   45°   90°   180°

3. Ethan wants to purchase a baseball bat for $12.00, a new mitt for $15.25, and a ball for $1.50. How much money does he need altogether to buy the items? _____

4.   45   5.   53   6.   122
       + 6   – 8   x 7

7. 8)‾3‾2‾

For questions 8–10, write how much time has passed.

8. 3:15 p.m. to 3:30 p.m. = _____ minutes

9. 4:15 a.m. to 4:25 a.m. = _____ minutes

10. 2:45 p.m. to 3:30 p.m. = _____ minutes

Fourth-Grade Math Minutes © 2002 Creative Teaching Press

MINUTE 12

NAME _____

1. 7)56

2. 6, 12, 18, 24, _____, _____

3. 68
  + 4

4. Circle the figure that is congruent to the shaded figure:

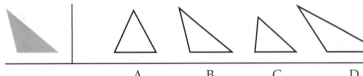

A   B   C   D

5. 45
  − 9

6. 23 − 8 =

7. 256
  x 4

In questions 8–10, does the figure have a line of symmetry? Write *yes* or *no*.
If yes, draw a line of symmetry.

8.  _____

9. _____

10. _____

MINUTE 13

NAME _____

1. 4 x 6 = 24   Which numbers are the <u>factors</u>? _____

2. 6)‾5‾4‾

3. The volume of the shape is 9 cubic centimeters.
Circle: True   or   False

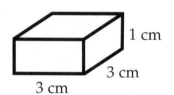
1 cm
3 cm
3 cm

4.   27
        + 7

length x width x height = volume

5. Harry bought a toy and a bag of treats for his cat. The total was $8.25. He paid with a ten-dollar bill. How much change did he receive? _____

6.   304   **7.**   32
        x   6   + 9

Use <, >, or = to complete questions 8–10.

8. 1 pint = 2 cups   5 pt _____ 10 c

9. 16 ounces = 1 pound   14 oz _____ 1 lb

10. 3 feet = 1 yard   21 ft _____ 7 yds

Fourth-Grade Math Minutes © 2002 Creative Teaching Press

MINUTE 14

NAME _____

1. 56
   − 8

2. 568
   x 7

3. 94
   + 6

4. Matthew has a 150-page book. He has read $\frac{1}{3}$ of it. How many pages has he read so far? _____ pages

5. 8)48

6. What is the <u>difference</u> of 5 and 7? _____

7. John has 24 cookies. He shares an equal number of cookies with 3 friends. How many cookies each do John and his friends get? _____ cookies

Use <, >, or = to complete questions 8–10.

8. 10 millimeters = 1 centimeter   5 mm _____ 1 cm

9. 1 meter = 100 centimeters   1m _____ 1 cm

10. 1 kilometer = 1,000 meters   1 km _____ 900 m

Fourth-Grade Math Minutes © 2002 Creative Teaching Press

MINUTE 15

NAME _____

1. The area of the shape is 6 square inches.
Circle: True   or   False

3 in.

3 in.

2.   244
    x 7

3.   85
    + 9

4. Claire earns $1.50 for each dog she walks for 15 minutes. Today, she walked two dogs for 15 minutes. How much money did she earn? _____

5. What is the <u>sum</u> of 10 and 12? _____

6.   91
    − 7

7.   9)‾54‾

For questions 8–10, write the equivalent fraction.

8. $\frac{8}{12}$ = ____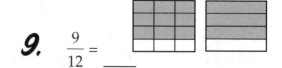

9. $\frac{9}{12}$ = ____

10. $\frac{4}{8}$ = ____

22

Fourth-Grade Math Minutes © 2002 Creative Teaching Press

MINUTE 16

NAME _____

1. Alice has 7 sheets of 20 stamps each. How many stamps does she have in all? _____ stamps

2. 7)̅4̅2̅   3.   75
                   + 8

4. $12 \div 3 = 4$ Which number is the <u>quotient</u>? _____

5. A <u>hex</u>agon has _____ sides and _____ angles.

6.   85   7.   645
    − 9   x 4

Use the circle graph to complete questions 8–10.

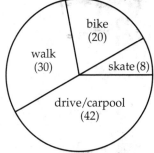

How Students Get to School

bike (20)
walk (30)
skate (8)
drive/carpool (42)

8. The greatest number of students get to school by _____.

9. The least number of students get to school by _____.

10. The sum of students who walk and bike to school is equal to the sum of students who _____ and _____ to school.

Fourth-Grade Math Minutes © 2002 Creative Teaching Press

MINUTE 17

NAME _____

1. 587
x 6

2. 5)30 (quotient 6) Which number is the <u>dividend</u>? _____

3. 93
+ 8

4. What is the perimeter of the shape? _____

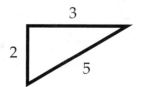

5. 7)49

6. The expanded form of 4,857 is _____ + _____ + _____ + _____.

7. 64
− 8

8. Chris has 7 wrenches and 4 screwdrivers.
How many tools does he have in all? _____ tools

For questions 9 and 10, circle the digit in the hundreds place.

9. 7,856

10. 945

Fourth-Grade Math Minutes © 2002 Creative Teaching Press

MINUTE 18

NAME _____

1. $5\overline{)35}$

2.
$$\begin{array}{r} 87 \\ +\ 6 \\ \hline \end{array}$$

3. 21 nickels = $_____

4. 35 + 25 =

5. A six-pack of juice sells for $3.60. How much does each juice cost? _____

6. 62 x 100 =

7.
$$\begin{array}{r} 515 \\ x\ \ 6 \\ \hline \end{array}$$

8. There are _____ minutes in 2 hours.

9.
$$\begin{array}{r} 85 \\ -\ 6 \\ \hline \end{array}$$

10. 18 ÷ 6 =

MINUTE 19

NAME _____

1. There are 8 puppies, and 3 of them have red collars. What fraction of the puppies have red collars? _____

2. Twelve is an even number.　　Circle:　True　or　False

3. 　86
　+ 6

4. 　4$\overline{)36}$

5. $2 \times 6 = 12$　Which number is the <u>product</u>? _____

6. The expanded form of 465 is _____ + _____ + _____.

7. 　642
　x　7

8. 　84
　− 8

For questions 9 and 10, write +, −, or x to make the sentence true.

9. $5 - 2$ _____ $3 = 6$

10. 4 _____ $3 + 8 = 20$

Fourth-Grade Math Minutes © 2002 Creative Teaching Press

MINUTE 20

NAME _____

1. 91
    − 6

2. 6⟌48

3. 5, 10, _____, 20, 25, 30

4. 7⟌35

5. 887
    + 7

6. $\overset{5}{3⟌15}$ Which number is the <u>divisor</u>? _____

7. 354
    x 6

For questions 8–10, round the number to the nearest hundred.

8. 621 _____

9. 548 _____

10. 584 _____

MINUTE 21

NAME _____

1. Mara has 7 pencils and Joy has 12 pencils. How many pencils do they have altogether? _____ pencils

2. Circle a reasonable measurement for the angle:
45°   90°   180°

3.   268
      + 14

In questions 4–6, what would you choose to measure each? Circle the answer.

4.   distance around a soccer field   centimeters   meters   kilometers

5.   width of a book   centimeters   meters   kilometers

6.   length of a baseball bat   centimeters   meters   kilometers

7.   618
      x   7

8. Identify the mean of the following numbers: 15, 18, 24. _____

For questions 9 and 10, write how much time has passed.

9. 5:00 a.m. to 6:25 a.m. = _____ hour(s) and _____ minutes

10. 8:15 p.m. to 9:30 p.m. = _____ hour(s) and _____ minutes

Fourth-Grade Math Minutes © 2002 Creative Teaching Press

MINUTE 22

NAME _____

1. 645
      − 28

2. 42 − 21 =

3. 645
      + 26

4. Circle the figure that is similar to the shaded figure:

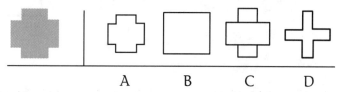

   A   B   C   D

5. 8⟌50

6. 8, 16, 24, 32, 40, _____, _____, _____

7. 542
      x 8

For questions 8–10, circle the name of the angle.

8. acute   right   obtuse

9. acute   right   obtuse

10. acute   right   obtuse

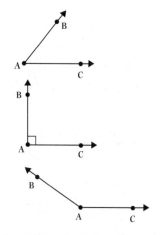

MINUTE 23

NAME _____

1. 7)‾45‾

2. 516
   − 33

3. The volume of the shape is _____ cubic centimeters.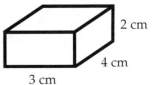

4. 862
   + 28

5. Mica bought a sandwich for $1.50, a soda for 50¢, and candy for 75¢. How much did he spend on lunch? _____

6. Identify the range of the following numbers: 7, 9, 15. _____

7. 941
   x 3

Use <, >, or = to complete questions 8–10.

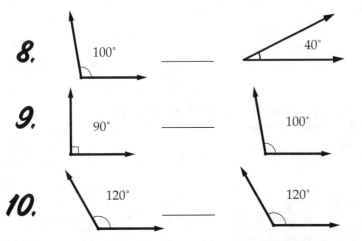

8. 100° _____ 40°

9. 90° _____ 100°

10. 120° _____ 120°

MINUTE 24

NAME _____

1. Gary has 12 tickets to the game. He gives away 8 tickets. How many tickets does he have left? _____ tickets

2. 847
   − 84

3. 7)$\overline{37}$

4. Chris had a tin of 24 cookies. He has eaten $\frac{1}{4}$ of the cookies. How many cookies has he eaten? _____ cookies

5. Identify the mode of the following numbers: 18, 4, 20, 25, 20. _____

6. 645
   + 78

7. 624
   x 7

8. $0.5 + 0.1 =$

For questions 9 and 10, write the value of the underlined digit.

9. $\underline{5}46 =$ _____

10. $94\underline{7} =$ _____

MINUTE 25

NAME _____

1. The area of the shape is _____ square inches.

3 in. [5 in.]

2. What is the <u>difference</u> of 8 and 22? _____

3. 6)‾38‾

4.   945
      + 94

5. 0.3 + 0.5 =

6.   845
      − 91

7.   879
      x   6

For questions 8–10, write the equivalent fraction.

8. $\frac{5}{10}$ = _____

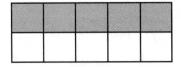

9. $\frac{2}{10}$ = _____

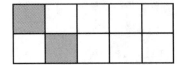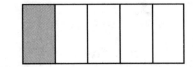

10. $\frac{6}{8}$ = _____

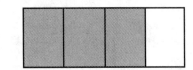

MINUTE 26

NAME _____

1. 954
      − 39

2. What is the <u>sum</u> of 4 and 12? _____

For questions 3 and 4, name the two right angles.

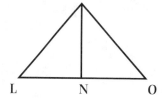

3. ∠ _____   **4.** ∠ _____

5. A <u>hep</u>tagon has _____ sides and _____ angles.

6. 7⟌67   **7.** 828
                    x 3

Use the bar graph to complete questions 8–10.

8. Which classroom collected the greatest number of cans? _____

9. How many cans did Room 12 collect? _____ cans

10. Which classroom collected 70 cans? _____

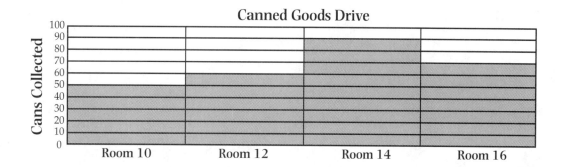

MINUTE 27

NAME _____

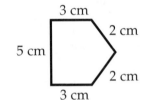

1. Write the fraction that names the shaded portions. _____

2. $3\overline{)24}$ with 8 above — Which number is the <u>quotient</u>? _____

3.
$$\begin{array}{r} 268 \\ + \ 14 \\ \hline \end{array}$$

4. The perimeter of the shape is _____ centimeters.

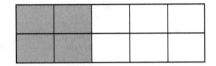

5. $8\overline{)60}$

6. The expanded form of 504 is _____.

7.
$$\begin{array}{r} 612 \\ - \ 81 \\ \hline \end{array}$$

8.
$$\begin{array}{r} 256 \\ \times \ \ 8 \\ \hline \end{array}$$

For questions 9 and 10, circle the digit in the thousands place.

9. 87,465

10. 4,974

Fourth-Grade Math Minutes © 2002 Creative Teaching Press

MINUTE 28

NAME _____

1. 24 ÷ 8 =

2. 875
   − 93

3. 40 nickels = _____ dimes

4. 758
   + 29

5. 547 x 100 =

6. There are 12 ice-cream cups in a box. If the box costs $9.60, how much does each cup of ice cream cost? _____

7. 654
   x   6

8. There are _____ minutes in $1\frac{1}{2}$ hours.

9. 17 + 42 =

10. 8)‾6‾8‾

35

MINUTE 29

NAME _____

1. Cara has 5 boxes with 100 sheets of paper in each. How many sheets of paper does she have in all? _____ sheets of paper

2. Twenty-three is an odd number.   Circle: True   or   False

3.   864
    − 84

4.   564   5.   9)‾48‾
    + 86

6. The expanded form of 845 is _____.

7.   232
    x   7

8. 24 ÷ 8 = 3   Which number is the dividend? _____

For question 9 and 10, write +, −, or x to make the sentence true.

9.   20 x 4 _____ 80 = 0

10.   100 x 100 _____ 1 = 10,001

MINUTE 30

NAME _____

1. 6 x 4 = 24   Which number is the <u>product</u>? _____

2.   846
       + 82

3.   7)‾55‾

4.   6, 12, _____, _____, 30, 36

5.   814
       − 53

6.   56 ÷ 8 =

7.   461
       x 9

For questions 8–10, round the number to the nearest ten.

8.   843 _____

9.   921 _____

10. 1,327 _____

MINUTE 31

NAME _____

1. 5,122
      x   7

2. Circle a reasonable measurement for the angle:

45°   90°   180°

3. Keith wants to purchase a football helmet for $35.00, shoulder pads for $10.00, and a football for $10.50. How much money does he need altogether to buy the items? _____

4. 7)168

5.   2,374
      + 3,135

6. 0.3 + 0.3 =

7.   842
      – 56

8. 24 ÷ 6 = 4   Which number is the <u>divisor</u>? _____

For questions 9 and 10, write how many hours have passed.

9. 11:15 p.m. to 1:15 a.m. = _____ hours

10. 10:15 a.m. to 1:15 p.m. = _____ hours

Excel! Grade 4 Math Minutes © 2009 Creative Teaching Press

MINUTE 32

NAME _____

1. 8)‾‾280‾‾   **2.**   6,208   **3.**   58 − 35 =
                    + 1,913

4. Circle the figure that is congruent to the shaded figure:

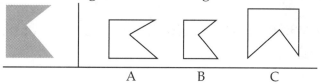

                    A   B   C

5. 10, 20, 30, _____, _____, _____

6.   785   **7.**   2,556
       − 96   x   4

For questions 8–10, circle the name of the geometric figure.

8.   ray   line   line segment

9.   radius   arc   angle

10. endpoint   face   plane

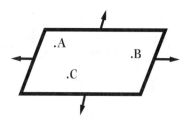

MINUTE 33

NAME _____

1. Identify the <u>mean</u> of the following numbers: 2, 4, 6, 8. _____

2. 821
    − 79

3. The volume of the shape is _____ cubic inches.

4 in.

10 in.

3 in.

For questions 4 and 5, circle the name of the angle.

4. acute   scalene   obtuse

5. acute   scalene   obtuse

6. Lila bought a sandwich for $5.25 and a soda for $1.75. She paid with a ten-dollar bill. How much change did she receive? _____

7. $6\overline{)270}$

Use <, >, or = to complete questions 8–10.

8. 945 _____ 954

9. 1,254 _____ 5,421

10. 542 _____ 425

MINUTE 34

NAME _____

1. 0.2 + 0.2 =

2.
```
  945
-  89
```

3. Identify the <u>range</u> of the following numbers: 12, 24, 14, 15, 26. _____

4. Brian has a box of 16 crayons. He takes half of the crayons out of the box. How many crayons are left in the box? _____ crayons

5.
```
  7,526
+ 2,484
```

6. Eric has 45 pieces of taffy. He gives all of them away by splitting them equally among his 3 brothers. How many pieces of taffy does each brother get? _____ pieces

7.
```
  8,568
x     7
```

8. 6)252

For questions 9 and 10, circle the value of the underlined digit.

9. 2.<u>1</u> =   1 one   1 tenth   1 hundredth

10. <u>2</u>.1 =   2 ones   2 tenths   2 hundredths

MINUTE 35

NAME _____

1. What is the perimeter of the shape? _____

2
8

2. 8)416

3. The abbreviation for centimeter is _____ .

4. Diana earns $3.50 for every hour of babysitting. If she babysits for 3 hours tonight, how much money will she earn? _____

5.
2,352
+ 1,292
_____

6. Identify the <u>mode</u> of the following numbers: 1, 6, 5, 6, 8. _____

7. Circle a reasonable measurement for the angle:
45°   90°   180°

For questions 8–10, write the equivalent fraction.

8. $\frac{2}{4}$ = _____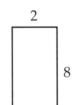

9. $\frac{2}{8}$ = _____

10. $\frac{2}{6}$ = _____

Fourth-Grade Math Minutes © 2002 Creative Teaching Press

MINUTE 36

NAME _____

1. There are 16 shells, and 4 of them are white. What fraction of the shells are white? _____

2. 6,545
   x   4

3. 2,671
   + 3,619

4. 7)441

5. An <u>octagon</u> has _____ sides and _____ angles.

6. What is the <u>difference</u> of 24 and 36? _____

7. What kind of angle is this? _____

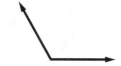

Use the bar graph to complete questions 8–10.

8. How many books did Room 16 read? _____ books

9. Which two classes read an equal number of books?
   _____

10. If there are 15 students in Room 12, what is the average number of books read per student? _____ books per student

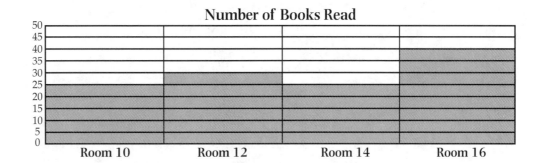

Number of Books Read

MINUTE 37

NAME _____

1. Write the fraction that names the shaded portion. _____

2. What is the <u>sum</u> of 15 and 12? _____

3.   3,614
     + 2,902

4. The perimeter of the shape is _____ inches.

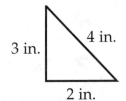

3 in.   4 in.

2 in.

5.   5,787
     x   6

6. The expanded form of 92,157 is
_____ + _____ + _____ + _____ + ___.

7.   862   **8.**   6)504
     – 84

For questions 9 and 10, circle the digit in the thousands place.

9.   74,865

10.   98,345

MINUTE 38

NAME _____

1. 7)‾49‾

2. 56 + 42 =

3. 12 quarters = _____ dollars

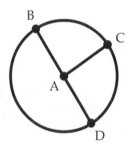

Use the circle to complete questions 4–6.

4. The center of the circle is _____ .

5. Three radii of the circle are $\overline{AB}$, _____, and _____ .

6. A diameter of the circle is _____ .

7. If a three-pack of blank videos costs $10.05, how much does each video cost? _____

8. There are _____ minutes in 3 hours.

9. 92 x 10 =   10. 7)‾392‾

MINUTE 39

NAME _____

1. $18 \div 3 = 6$ Which number is the <u>quotient</u>? _____

2. Twenty-one is an even number.   Circle: True or False

3. $0.4 + 0.2 =$

4.
$$\begin{array}{r} 847 \\ -\ 59 \\ \hline \end{array}$$

5.
$$\begin{array}{r} 8,915 \\ +\ 3,805 \\ \hline \end{array}$$

6. The expanded form of 2,804 is _____.

7.
$$\begin{array}{r} 6,642 \\ \times\ \ \ 7 \\ \hline \end{array}$$

8. $6\overline{)2,712}$

For questions 9 and 10, write +, −, or x to make the sentence true.

9. 4×2 _____ $2 = 16$

10. 5×6 _____ $5 = 25$

Fourth-Grade Math Minutes © 2002 Creative Teaching Press

MINUTE 40

NAME _____

1. $35 \div 7 = 5$ Which number is the dividend? _____

2.   846
        − 38

3. A pentagon has _____ sides and _____ angles.

4. 16, _____, 32, 40, 48, 54

5.   8,465
        + 8,165

6. $48 \div 6 =$

7.   7,354
        x   6

For questions 8–10, round the number to the nearest hundred.

8. 136 _____

9. 845 _____

10. 854 _____

Fourth-Grade Math Minutes © 2002 Creative Teaching Press

MINUTE 41

NAME _____

1. 3 x 4 = 12   Which number is the product? _____

2. Circle a reasonable measurement for the angle:
   30°   90°   120°

3. Pia wants to purchase a pair of in-line skates for $30.50, a pair of knee pads for $8.25, and a pair of wrist guards for $10.00. How much money does she need altogether to buy the items? _____

4. 20)‾40‾

5. 7,945
   + 6,852

6. 120
   x 17

7. 2,948
   −   487

8. Max walks 2 dogs. Ben walks 3 dogs. Milo walks 5 dogs. How many dogs do they walk altogether? _____ dogs

For questions 9 and 10, write how much time has passed.

9. 4:15 a.m. to 6:25 a.m. = _____ hours and _____ minutes

10. 7:15 p.m. to 10:45 p.m. = _____ hours and _____ minutes

Fourth-Grade Math Minutes © 2002 Creative Teaching Press

MINUTE 42

NAME _____

1. 9)81

2. 9,645
   + 7,312

3. 91 – 50 =

4. Circle the figure that is similar to the shaded figure:

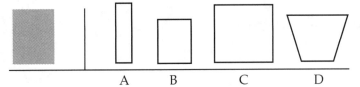

A   B   C   D

5. 6, 9, 12, 15, 18, _____, _____, _____

6. 206
   x 14

7. 9,345
   – 585

In questions 8–10, does the figure have a line of symmetry? Write *yes* or *no*.
If yes, draw the line of symmetry.

8.  _____

9. _____

10. _____

MINUTE 43

NAME _____

1. $7\overline{)21}$ with 3 above   Which number is the <u>divisor</u>? _____

2.   8,638
      − 758

3. The volume of the shape is _____ cubic centimeters.

10 cm
2 cm
2 cm

4.   4,615
      + 9,375

5. Gus bought a bag of sweet corn for $5.50 and a stick of butter for $0.50. He paid with a twenty-dollar bill. How much change did he receive? _____

6. Write the fraction that names the shaded portions.

_____

7. $14\overline{)56}$

Use <, >, or = to complete questions 8–10.

8. 11 in. _____ 1 ft

9. 2 lbs _____ 22 oz

10. 2 qt _____ 16 pt

MINUTE 44

NAME _____

1. 13$\overline{)39}$

2. 3,497
    − 595

3. 8,613
    + 5,916

4. Maya has 6 pairs of shorts, and $\frac{1}{3}$ of them are blue. How many blue shorts does she own? _____ blue shorts

5. Identify the <u>mean</u> of the following numbers: 50, 100, 150. _____

6. 0.5 + 0.1 =

7. 508
    x 17

Use <, >, or = to complete questions 8–10.

8. 1 kg _____ 1000 g

9. 1 g _____ 500 kg

10. 200 g _____ $\frac{1}{2}$ kg

MINUTE 45

NAME _____

1. The area of the shape is _____ square inches.

6 in.

9 in.

2. 11$\overline{)66}$

3. 7,615
− 807

4. There are 12 pencils in a box, and each pencil costs one nickel. If Henry wants to buy the whole box, how much money does he need? _____

5. 7,107
+ 3,987

6. 214
x 17

7. Identify the <u>range</u> of the following numbers: 50, 100, 150. _____

For questions 8–10, write the equivalent fraction.

8. $\frac{4}{6}$ = _____

9. $\frac{9}{18}$ = _____

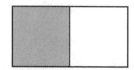 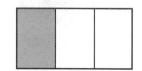

10. $\frac{6}{18}$ = _____

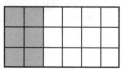

Fourth-Grade Math Minutes © 2002 Creative Teaching Press

MINUTE 46

NAME _____

1. 15)‾60‾   **2.** 222   **3.** 8,685   **4.** 7,641
                  x 14   – 758   + 3,948

5. A pentagon has _____ sides and _____ angles.

6. Identify the <u>mode</u> of the following numbers: 9, 18, 5, 6, 6. _____

7. Judi has 53 stickers. She gives 13 to her best friend. How many stickers does Judi have left? _____ stickers

Use the line graph to complete questions 8–10.

8. Two days a week, Josh's only chore is to take the dog on a walk. Which two days of the week are most likely these days?

_____

9. One day a week, Josh must do his own chores and help his family clean. Which day is most likely the family's cleaning day?

_____

10. On which day does Josh not do chores? _____

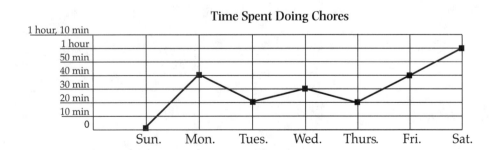

MINUTE 47

NAME _____

1. Write the fraction that names the shaded portions. _____

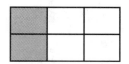

2. 11$\overline{)88}$ 3.   8,695
                              − 786

4. The perimeter of the shape is _____ feet.

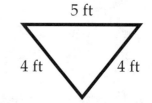

5 ft

4 ft   4 ft

5.   3,915
     + 7,968

6. The expanded form of 6,543 is _____.

7.   522
     x 16

8. What is the difference of 32 and 40? _____

For questions 9 and 10, circle the digit in the tens place.

9. 76,849

10. 54,865

MINUTE 48

NAME _____

1. 212 x 10 =

2. 56 ÷ 8 =

3. 20 nickels = _____ dimes

4. 51 + 38 =

5. 4,357
   + 3,862

6. Joanie is buying dog treats for the animal shelter. Brand A is on sale for two boxes for $4.50. Brand B is on sale for $2.50 each. Which brand has the better deal? _____

7. 2,693
   − 689

8. There are _____ minutes in 4 hours.

9. 515
   x 16

10. 14)‾42‾

MINUTE 49

NAME _____

1. There are 42 pairs of shoes at the skate rental office. How many individual shoes are there in all? _____ individual shoes

2. Thirty-eight is an odd number.   Circle: True   or   False

3. What is the <u>sum</u> of 54 and 20? _____

4. $17\overline{)68}$ 5.   6,758
                                   + 8,624

6. The expanded form of 2,085 is _____.

7.   3,922
    − 841

8.   642
    x 17

For questions 9 and 10, write +, −, or x to make the sentence true.

9. 20 x 10 _____ 10 = 190

10. 2 x 30 _____ 60 = 120

Fourth-Grade Math Minutes © 2002 Creative Teaching Press

MINUTE 50

NAME _____

1. $40 \div 8 = 5$ Which number is the <u>quotient</u>? _____

2.
$$
\begin{array}{r}
8{,}238 \\
-\ 546 \\
\hline
\end{array}
$$

3.
$$
\begin{array}{r}
8{,}768 \\
+\ 3{,}531 \\
\hline
\end{array}
$$

4. $24 \div 8 =$

5. 21, _____, 35, 42, _____, 56, 63

6.
$$
\begin{array}{r}
312 \\
\times\ 23 \\
\hline
\end{array}
$$

7. $30\overline{)60}$

For questions 8–10, round the number to the nearest thousand.
Circle the answer.

8. 1,849 rounds to _____   1,000   2,000

9. 2,448 rounds to _____   2,000   3,000

10. 3,894 rounds to _____   3,000   4,000

MINUTE 51

NAME _____

1. Bailey has 49 dog treats and 7 dogs. If she gives each dog a single treat each day, how many days will her treats last? _____ days

2. Circle a reasonable measurement for the angle:
30°   90°   120°

3. 15)‾180

4. Lester has a new dirt bike. He wants to purchase a helmet for $115.00, a pair of motocross pants for $50.00, and new gloves for $12.00. How much money does he need altogether to buy the items? _____

5.   7,823
       + 9,435

6.   112
       x 27

7.   3,054
       − 948

8. Which point is at (3, 2)?

_____

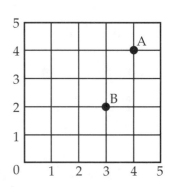

For questions 9 and 10, write how many hours have passed.

9. 8:10 p.m. to 3:10 a.m. = _____ hours

10. 9:00 a.m. to 2:00 p.m. = _____ hours

Fourth-Grade Math Minutes © 2002 Creative Teaching Press

MINUTE 52

NAME _____

For questions 1 and 2, solve the problem. There are no remainders.

1. $15\overline{)120}$ **2.** $17\overline{)119}$ **3.** $65 - 42 =$

4. Circle the figure that is congruent to the shaded figure:

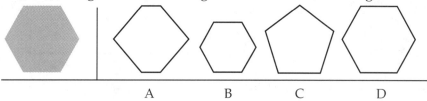

        A   B   C   D

5. Forty-three is an even number.   Circle: True   or   False

6. 15, 20, 25, 30, _____, _____, _____   **7.**   4,899
                                                               − 687

For questions 8–10, underline the best name of the figure.

8. ray   line   line segment

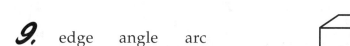

9. edge   angle   arc

10. face   point   plane

MINUTE 53

NAME _____

1. 19)285

2. Evan has a 10-page report to write. If he has already written 4 pages, what fraction of the report has he written? _____

3. The volume of the shape is _____ cubic centimeters.

4.
8,782
+ 8,184

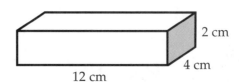
2 cm
4 cm
12 cm

5. Celia bought four apples for $0.50 each. She paid with a five-dollar bill. How much change did she receive? _____

6.
635
x 35

7.
7,538
– 617

Use <, >, or = to complete questions 8–10.

8. _____

9. _____

10. _____

MINUTE 54

NAME _____

1. Lacey and Jake each have a pair of skates with four wheels on each skate. How many wheels do they have altogether? _____ wheels

2.
```
  126
x  55
```

3. $14\overline{)210}$

4. Josh has 12 computer games. He received $\frac{1}{4}$ of them for his birthday. How many computer games did he receive for his birthday? _____ games

5.
```
  5,315
+ 3,948
```

6. $1.2 + 2.3 =$

7. Ninety-seven is an odd number.   Circle: True   or   False

8. $\frac{1}{3} + \frac{1}{3} =$

For questions 9 and 10, write the value of the underlined digit.

9. 6.3 = _____

10. 5.45 = _____

Fourth-Grade Math Minutes © 2002 Creative Teaching Press

MINUTE 55

NAME _____

1. The area of the shape is _____ square inches.

30 in.

10 in.

2. 849
      x 56

3. 16)‾320‾

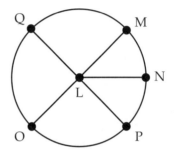

Use the circle to complete questions 4–6.

4. The center is _____ .

5. Two diameters are $\overline{QP}$ and _____ .

6. Five radii are $\overline{LO}$, $\overline{LQ}$, _____, _____, and _____.

7. Cooper has 35 sports cards. He gives 14 to a friend. How many cards does Cooper have left? _____ cards

For questions 8–10, write the equivalent fraction.

8. $\dfrac{1}{2} = \dfrac{\square}{4}$

9. 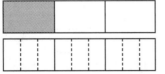 $\dfrac{1}{3} = \dfrac{\square}{9}$

10. 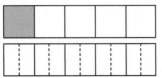 $\dfrac{1}{5} = \dfrac{\square}{10}$

Fourth-Grade Math Minutes © 2002 Creative Teaching Press

MINUTE 56

NAME _____

1. 16)‾144‾   **2.** A <u>line</u> has two endpoints.   Circle: True   or   False

3. Montana needs 40 chocolate pieces for her recipe. If each chocolate bar has 8 pieces, how many chocolate bars does she need? _____ bars

4. This figure is ray $\overrightarrow{NM}$.   M •———• N   Circle: True   or   False

5. A <u>hex</u>agon has _____ sides and _____ angles.   **6.**   342
                                                                              x 65

7. 1.2 + 0.5 =

Use the bar graph to complete questions 8–10.

8. Which two students swam the greatest number of laps?

_____

9. Students had to swim a minimum number of laps. Four students swam only the minimum. What was the minimum number of laps? _____ laps

10. Who swam the greater number of laps: Jake or Zoe? _____

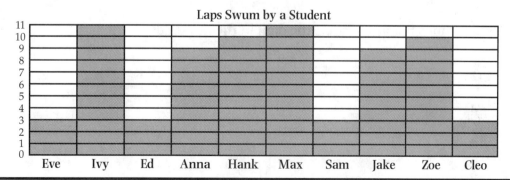

Laps Swum by a Student

63

MINUTE 57

NAME _____

1. Marco wants to make 8 cookies for each of his 8 cousins. How many cookies does he need to make in all? _____ cookies

2. The letter B is symmetrical.   Circle: True   or   False

3. $\dfrac{2}{3} - \dfrac{1}{3} =$

4. The perimeter of the shape is _____ cm.

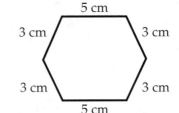

5.   8,097
    + 5,035
    _____

6. The expanded form of 8,402 is _____.

For questions 7 and 8, name a decimal for the fraction. Circle the answer.

7. $\dfrac{6}{10} =$ _____   0.6   0.06

8. $\dfrac{2}{100} =$ _____   0.2   0.02

For questions 9 and 10, circle the digit in the hundreds place.

9. 9,457

10. 8,978

MINUTE 58

NAME _____

1. $42 \div 7 =$

2. 12 nickels = _____ dimes

3. LaDawn buys a ten-pack of gel pens for $7.50. How much did each pen cost? _____

For questions 4–6, name a fraction for the decimal. Circle the answer.

4. $0.5 =$ _____ $\dfrac{5}{1}$ $\dfrac{5}{10}$ $\dfrac{5}{100}$

5. $0.06 =$ _____ $\dfrac{6}{10}$ $\dfrac{6}{100}$ $\dfrac{60}{100}$

6. $0.9 =$ _____ $\dfrac{9}{1}$ $\dfrac{9}{10}$ $\dfrac{9}{100}$

7. $37 + 22 =$

8. There are _____ minutes in 120 seconds.

9. $16 \overline{)208}$ 10. $905 \times 100 =$

65

MINUTE 59

NAME _____

1. There are 15 cats. If 5 of the cats are striped, what fraction of the cats are striped? _____

2. Thirty-eight is an even number.   Circle: True   or   False

3. 3.2 + 0.5 =

4.   8,760
        + 3,864

5. The expanded form of 54,822 is

_____ + _____ + _____ + _____ + ___.

For questions 6 and 7, name a decimal for the fraction. Circle the answer.

6. $\frac{8}{100}$ = _____   8.0   0.8   0.08

7. $\frac{75}{100}$ = _____   75.0   7.5   0.75

8. $11\overline{)110}$

For questions 9 and 10, write +, −, or x to make the sentence true.

9.   15 + 5 _____ 5 = 15

10.   69 ÷ 3 _____ 1 = 24

MINUTE 60

NAME _____

1. There are 40 books on the first bookshelf and 55 books on the second bookshelf. How many books are there in all? _____ books

2. 40 ÷ 8 =

For questions 3–5, name the decimal for the written fraction. Circle the answer.

3. two tenths   0.2   0.02   2.0

4. one and eight hundredths   1.8   1.08   0.18

5. five and six tenths   5.6   5.06   .56

6. 27, _____, 45, 54, 63, 72, _____, 90   **7.** 13)‾221‾

For questions 8–10, round the number to the nearest hundred.

8. 754 _____

9. 745 _____

10. 475 _____

MINUTE 61

NAME _____

1. 12)‾192

2. Circle a reasonable measurement for the angle:
30°   90°   120°

3. Daniela wants to buy a basketball for $15.00 and a new pair of sneakers for $75.50. How much money does she need altogether to buy the items?

_____

4. Ryan has 25 marbles. He gives away 8 marbles. How many marbles does he have left? _____ marbles

For questions 5–7, circle the best answer for each.

5. An insect is about _____ long.   1 yd   1 ft   1 in.

6. Tyler rode his bicycle _____ in 30 minutes.   4 mi   400 yd   2,000 ft

7. The height of a telephone pole is about _____ tall.   10 ft   1 yd   24 in.

8. Which point is at (2, 2)? _____

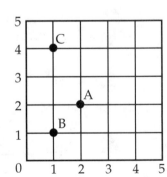

For questions 9 and 10, write how many hours have passed.

9. 7:15 a.m. to 4:15 p.m. = _____

10. 5:30 p.m. to 3:30 a.m. = _____

MINUTE 62

NAME _____

1. 16)̅1̅7̅6̅   **2.**   21, 28, 35, 42, _____, _____, _____

3.   2,145
      x   23

4. Circle the figure that is similar to the shaded figure:

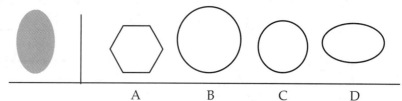

         A   B   C   D

In questions 5 and 6, what would you choose to measure each? Circle the answer.

5. height of an adult   inch   foot   yard   mile

6. length of the Colorado River   inch   foot   yard   mile

7. 65 – 53 =

For questions 8–10, circle the the name of the triangle.

8. equilateral   isosceles   scalene

9. equilateral   isosceles   scalene

10. equilateral   isosceles   scalene

MINUTE 63

NAME _____

1. Gabe has 4 packages of batteries. There are 10 batteries in each package. How many batteries does he have in all? _____ batteries

2. 234
x 32

3. The volume of the shape is _____ cubic inches.

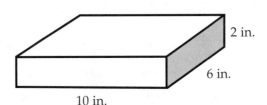

2 in.

6 in.

10 in.

4. Jason bought a movie ticket for $5.50 and popcorn for $3.35. How much did he spend? _____

5. 16⟌160

6. An equilateral triangle has only two congruent sides.
Circle: True   or   False

7. The expanded form of 56,492 is

_____ .

Use <, >, or = to complete questions 8–10.

8. 5,645 _____ 4,655

9. 498 _____ 489

10. 546 _____ 645

MINUTE 64

NAME _____

1. $18\overline{)252}$

2. There are 81 butterflies altogether. There are only 9 types of butterflies. If there are an equal number of each type of butterfly, how many butterflies are there of each type? _____ butterflies

3. 216
x 35

4. Kyra has a box of 42 chocolates. If $\frac{1}{6}$ of the box are caramels, how many caramels are in the box? _____ caramels

5. A right triangle has exactly one right angle.
Circle: True   or   False

6. $\frac{1}{4} + \frac{2}{4} =$

7. Lines that never cross are called <u>parallel</u>.   Circle: True   or   False

8. 2.5 + 5.4 =

For questions 9 and 10, write the value of the underlined digit.

9. 8.<u>5</u>4 = _____

10. 8.5<u>4</u> = _____

MINUTE 65

NAME _____

1. The area of the shape is _____ square centimeters.

24 cm

8 cm

2. There are 30 students, and 6 of them wear sandals. What fraction of the students wear sandals? _____

3. Lines that cross are called <u>intersecting</u>.   Circle: True   or   False

4. There are 15 collector cards in a package, and each card is $0.15. If Ed wants to buy the whole package, how much money does he need? _____

5.   94,685
     + 4,058

6.   13)‾234‾

7. The name of the circle is _____ .

For questions 8–10, write the equivalent fraction.

8. $\frac{1}{3} = \frac{2}{6} = \frac{\Box}{12}$

9. $\frac{1}{4} = \frac{2}{8} = \frac{\Box}{16}$

10. $\frac{1}{2} = \frac{2}{4} = \frac{\Box}{12}$

MINUTE 66

NAME _____

1. There are 9 wolf spiders and 18 house spiders. How many spiders are there in all? _____ spiders

Use <, >, or = to complete questions 2 and 3.

2. 2 quarters and 5 dimes _____ $1.00

3. 1 half-dollar and 4 dimes _____ $0.88

4. 2.4 + 1.3 =

5. All squares are rectangles. Circle: True or False

6. $13\overline{)143}$

7. Lines that intersect at right angles are called <u>parallel</u>.
   Circle: True or False

Use the line graph to complete questions 8–10.

8. Which month had the greatest number of birthdays?_____

9. Which two months each had three birthdays?
   _____

10. Are there more birthdays from January to June or from July to December?
    _____

Students' Birthdays

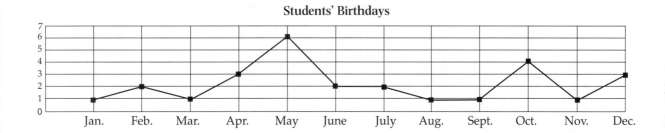

MINUTE 67

NAME _____

1. Write the fraction that names the shaded portions. _____

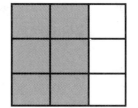

2. 41,098
  + 64,502

3. 321
  x 36

4. What is the perimeter of the shape? _____

15

8   8

10

5. 17)‾306‾

6. The expanded form of 40,054 is _____.

7. A <u>ray</u> is a part of a line with one endpoint.   Circle: True   or   False

8. There are 12 wolves in the pack, and 3 grow up and leave the pack. How many wolves remain in the pack? _____ wolves

For questions 9 and 10, circle the digit in the thousands place.

9. 74,165

10. 86,495

Fourth-Grade Math Minutes © 2002 Creative Teaching Press

MINUTE 68

NAME _____

1. 64 ÷ 8 =   **2.** 56 + 33 =

3. 20 dimes and 8 nickels = $_____

4. A line segment is straight and has _____ endpoints.

5.
$$
\begin{array}{r}
244 \\
\times\ 33 \\
\hline
\end{array}
$$

6. Sherri buys a bag of 100 rubber bands for $3.00. How much does each rubber band cost? _____

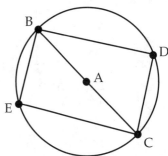

Use the figure to complete questions 7 and 8.

7. Name the diameter. _____

8. Name two triangles. _____ _____

9. 725 x 1,000 =

10. 17)‾204‾

MINUTE 69

NAME _____

1. There are 3 tractors with 4 wheels each and 4 tractors with 8 wheels each. How many wheels are there in all? _____ wheels

2. Forty-five is an odd number.   Circle: True   or   False

3. $18\overline{)360}$

4. The expanded form of 20,850 is _____.

For questions 5–7, circle the correct decimal.

5. two and two tenths   20.0   2.0   2.2   0.02

6. forty-two hundredths   0.42   4.20   0.042   420.0

7. three and one hundredth   310.0   31.0   3.10   3.01

8. $\dfrac{7}{8} - \dfrac{2}{8} =$ _____

For questions 9 and 10, write +, –, or x to make the sentence true.

9. $60 \div 3$ _____ $4 = 80$

10. $24 \div 6$ _____ $22 = 88$

Fourth Grade Math Minutes © 2002 Creative Teaching Press

MINUTE 70

NAME _____

1. $35 \div 7 =$

2. $\dfrac{37}{5} = 7\dfrac{\boxed{}}{5}$

3. Write the decimal 9.1 in words. _____

4. 18, 24, _____, 36, _____, 48, 54

5. The distance around a figure is called the _____.
   length   area   perimeter   width

6. $18\overline{)306}$ 7. $\begin{array}{r} 7,504 \\ -\,2,448 \\ \hline \end{array}$

For questions 8–10, round the number to the nearest thousand.

8. 43,159 _____

9. 34,195 _____

10. 43,951 _____

Fourth-Grade Math Minutes © 2002 Creative Teaching Press

MINUTE 71

NAME _____

1. Write seven and four tenths as a decimal. _____

2. Circle a reasonable measurement for the angle:
   30°   180°   210°

3.   7,058
    x   35

4. Nathan buys two baseball tickets for $15.00 each and two lunches for $3.50 each. How much money does he spend altogether? _____

5. A letter weighs about _____.
   4 g   40 g   4 kg

6.   14⟌168

7. $\frac{45}{7} = 6\frac{\Box}{7}$

8. Which point is at (2, 3)? _____

In questions 9 and 10, what would you choose to measure each? Circle the answer.

9. a coffee cup   liter   milliliter

10. a gasoline tank   liter   milliliter

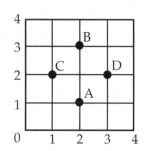

MINUTE 72

NAME _____

1. 15⟌300   **2.** 27, 36, 45, 54, _____, _____, _____   **3.** 102
                                                                       x 47

4. Circle the figure that is congruent to the shaded figure:

     A   B   C   D

For questions 5 and 6, circle *liters* or *milliliters* to complete each sentence.

5. The parrot drank about 7 _____ of water.   liters   milliliters

6. The swimming pool holds about 40,000 _____ of water.   liters   milliliters

7. 67 – 43 =

In questions 8–10, does the figure have a line of symmetry? Write *yes* or *no*.
If yes, draw a line of symmetry.

8. ⇕ _____

9. ☆ _____

10. 🚫 _____

MINUTE 73

NAME _____

For questions 1 and 2, write the degree Fahrenheit (°F) temperature.

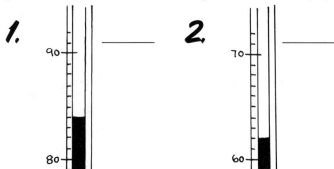

1. _____   **2.** _____

3. The volume of the shape is _____ cubic inches.

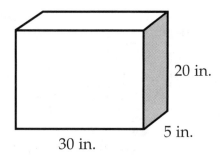

20 in.

30 in.   5 in.

4. 45,098
      + 59,405

5. Helen and Emily each bought two cookies for $0.50 each, and they shared a carton of milk that cost $1.75. How much did they spend altogether? _____

6. The expanded form of 89,025 is _____ .

7. There are 15 mother hens. If each hen lays 10 eggs a week, how many eggs will the hens lay altogether each week? _____ eggs

Use <, >, or = to complete questions 8–10.

8. 12 in. _____ 1 ft   **9.** 7 yds _____ 20 ft   **10.** 2 lbs _____ 23 oz

Fourth-Grade Math Minutes © 2002 Creative Teaching Press

MINUTE 74

NAME _____

1. 6.2 + 3.1 = _____

2. Linus has a jar of 120 jelly beans. If $\frac{1}{8}$ of the jelly beans are green, how many green jelly beans are in the jar? _____ green jelly beans

For questions 3–5, write the decimal.

3. $\frac{24}{100}$ _____

4. $2\frac{3}{10}$ _____

5. $1\frac{9}{100}$ _____

6. $\frac{38}{9} = 4\frac{\boxed{}}{9}$

7. $21\overline{)9{,}492}$

Use <, >, or = to complete questions 8–10.

8. 1 m _____ 650 cm

9. 1 km _____ 1500 m

10. 100 g _____ 1 kg

MINUTE 75

NAME _____

14 cm

14 cm

1. The area of the shape is _____ square centimeters.

2. Three children are playing. Four children join them. Five others join the group. How many children are now playing? _____ children

3. 3.09 > 3.9   Circle: True   or   False

4. Grace earns $3.50 an hour at the library. If she works for 4 hours, how much money does she earn? _____

For questions 5 and 6, write the degree Celsius (°C) temperature.

5. 40 ___ 30 20   _____

6. 100 90 80   _____

7. $35\overline{)4,340}$

For questions 8–10, write the equivalent fraction.

8. $\dfrac{9}{12} = \dfrac{\square}{4}$

9. $\dfrac{6}{9} = \dfrac{\square}{3}$

10. $\dfrac{4}{10} = \dfrac{\square}{5}$

Fourth-Grade Math Minutes © 2002 Creative Teaching Press

MINUTE 76

NAME _____

1. Henry draws 15 pictures. He gives his 2 aunts 4 pictures each. How many pictures does he have left? _____ pictures

2. $\dfrac{37}{5} = 7\dfrac{\square}{\square}$

3. $8.9 - 3.6 =$

4. $\dfrac{1}{4}$ of $20 =$

5. A _____ is a parallelogram with four equal sides.

For questions 6 and 7, write the decimals from least to greatest.

6. 5.25   5.32   5.3   _____

7. 0.2   0.02   2.02   _____

Use the line graph to complete questions 8–10.

8. Which month received the greatest amount of rainfall?
   _____

9. Did the amount of rainfall increase or decrease from October to December? _____

10. September and _____ each received 0.3 inches of rainfall.

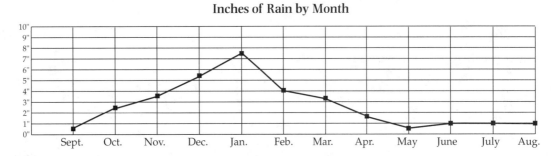

Inches of Rain by Month

MINUTE 77

NAME _____

1. If 3 cats each catch 12 mice, how many mice have they caught altogether? _____ mice

2. $\dfrac{28}{3} = 9\dfrac{\square}{\square}$

3. 4.62 < 4.67   Circle: True   or   False

4. What is the perimeter of the shape?_____

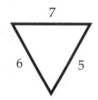

5. 16,945
+ 65,093

6. The expanded form of 4,602 is _____.

For questions 7 and 8, write the time.

7. 30 minutes after 8:35 p.m.   _____

8. 1 hour and 15 minutes after 2:20 p.m. _____

For questions 9 and 10, circle the digit in the ten thousands place.

9. 74,086

10. 65,804

Fourth-Grade Math Minutes © 2002 Creative Teaching Press

MINUTE 78

NAME _____

1. The expanded form of 45,029 is _____ + _____ + _____ + ____ .

2. 29 + 21 =

3. 35 dimes = $_____

For questions 4 and 5, write the decimals in order from greatest to least.

4. 2.5   1.8   3.2   _____

5. 10.4   11.5   1.5   _____

6. Carla buys a bag of 12 apples for $1.44. How much is each apple worth? _____

7. How many minutes are there in 240 seconds? _____ minutes

8. 65 x 1,000 =

9.   5,842
       − 3,034

10. $\frac{5}{8} + \frac{2}{8} =$

Fourth-Grade Math Minutes © 2002 Creative Teaching Press

MINUTE 79

NAME _____

1. $\dfrac{5}{6} - \dfrac{2}{6} =$

2. Forty-five is an even number.   Circle: True   or   False

3. 6.4 + 2.5 =

4. $\dfrac{31}{4} = 7\dfrac{\Box}{\Box}$ 5.   8.4 – 7.2 =

6. The expanded form of 70,804 is _____.

7. $5\overline{)350}$

8. 105, 110, 115, _____ , _____ , _____

For questions 9 and 10, write +, –, or x to make the sentence true.

9. 45 ÷ 3 _____ 5 = 20

10. 36 ÷ 12 _____ 3 = 6

MINUTE 80

NAME _____

1. $8\overline{)48}$

2. $\dfrac{53}{6} = \square\,\dfrac{\square}{\square}$

3. $12.7 - 6.4 =$

4. 28, 35, _____, 49, _____, 63, 70

5. $12 \times 5 =$ 6. $42\overline{)9,744}$

7.   4 qt = 1 gal
   _____ qt = 6 gal

For questions 8–10, round the number to the nearest ten.

8. 345 _____

9. 478 _____

10. 464 _____

MINUTE 81

NAME _____

1. Circle a reasonable measurement for the angle:
30°   180°   210°

2. Claudia bought lunch for her friends. She bought three cheeseburgers for $3.00 each and three sodas for $1.25 each. How much did she spend?
_____

For questions 3–5, circle what you would use to measure each.

3. a large pitcher of punch   cup   pint   quart   gallon

4. a small bowl of soup   cup   pint   quart   gallon

5. a swimming pool   cup   pint   quart   gallon

6. Which point is at (1, 2)? _____

7.
```
   20,945
 - 15,497
```

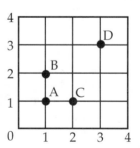

For questions 8–10, circle the most reasonable temperature.

8. making a snowman   15°F   48°F   70°F

9. swimming on a summer day   38°F   60°F   82°F

10. wearing a sweatshirt outdoors   40°F   65°F   78°F

MINUTE 82

NAME _____

1. The temperature inside of a freezer is about 210°F. Circle: True or False

2. _____, _____, _____, 24, 30, 36, 42, 48

3. 615
   x 125

4. Circle the figure that is similar to the shaded figure:

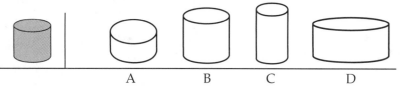

   A   B   C   D

5. 12.9   6. $\frac{45}{8}$ = ☐ ☐/☐   7. 35,984
   – 2.2   – 15,978

For questions 8–10, circle the name of the geometric figure.

8. ray   line   line segment

9. radius   arc   diameter

10. endpoint   plane   edge

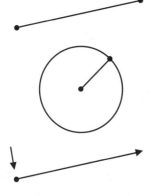

MINUTE 83

NAME _____

1. Two faces on a solid figure meet at an edge.   Circle: True   or   False

2. Casey bought two Popsicles for $1.75 each and a juice box for $1.50. He paid with a ten-dollar bill. How much change did he receive? _____

3. The perimeter of the shape is _____ cm.

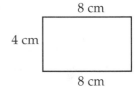

4. $\begin{array}{r} 10.5 \\ -\ 8.1 \\ \hline \end{array}$ **5.** $\begin{array}{r} 62,705 \\ +\ 20,097 \\ \hline \end{array}$ **6.** $\begin{array}{r} 54,978 \\ -\ 29,877 \\ \hline \end{array}$

7. $\dfrac{45}{8} =$

Use <, >, or = to complete questions 8–10.

8.  15° _____   345°

9. 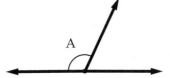 _____

10.  45° _____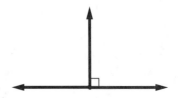

90

MINUTE 84

NAME _____

1. $\frac{13}{4} =$

2. $2.4 - 1.2 =$

3. Joe is sorting his family's clean socks. He has 90 individual socks, and $\frac{1}{5}$ of those are blue. How many socks are blue? _____ blue socks

4. Look at question #3. How many pairs of blue socks are there? _____ pairs

5. A diameter doesn't pass through the center of a circle. Circle: True or False

For questions 6 and 7, circle what you would use to measure each.

6. distance across an ocean   foot   yard   mile

7. weight of a train engine   ounce   pound   ton

8. $\frac{6}{9} + \frac{1}{9} =$

For questions 9 and 10, write the value of the underlined digit.

9. $8.\underline{9}4 =$ _____

10. $\underline{92}.74 =$ _____

Fourth-Grade Math Minutes © 2002 Creative Teaching Press

MINUTE 85

NAME _____

1. What is the area of the shape?_____

8 ⌐──────── 16 ────────┐
  │   │
  └────────────────────┘

2. 845
    x 21

3. There are 10 reams of paper in a box, and each ream is $4.00. Carla wants to buy half of the box. How much money will she need? _____

4. $19.4 + 6.2 =$

5. 54,316
   + 80,316

6. $\dfrac{19}{3} =$

7. The expanded form of 512,007 is _____ + _____ + _____ + _____.

For questions 8–10, write the equivalent fraction.

8. $\dfrac{5}{25} = \dfrac{}{5}$

9. $\dfrac{6}{30} = \dfrac{}{5}$

10. $\dfrac{6}{18} = \dfrac{}{3}$

MINUTE 86

NAME _____

1.   62,498
      − 52,977

2.   2.25 + 3.56 =

3.   74,805
      + 82,065

4. $\frac{37}{5}$ =

5. $\frac{3}{8} + \frac{4}{8}$ =

For questions 6 and 7, circle what you would use to weigh each.

6.   a helicopter   g   kg

7.   a hot dog   g   kg

Use the line graph to complete questions 8–10.

8.   Which day had the lowest high temperature?
     _____

9.   On which day was it 77°? _____

10.   Did the temperature increase or decrease from Monday to Tuesday?
     _____

High Temperature by Day

Temp	Sun.	Mon.	Tues.	Wed.	Thurs.	Fri.	Sat.
77°							■
76°							
75°		■				■	
74°				■			
73°			■		■		
72°							
71°	■						

MINUTE 87

NAME _____

1. Write the fraction that names the shaded portions. _____

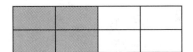

For questions 2 and 3, circle what you would use to measure how much each holds.

2. a bathtub   mL   L

3. a tea cup   mL   L

4. What is the perimeter of the shape? _____

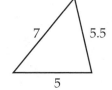

7

5.5

5

5. $\frac{2}{6} + \frac{3}{6} =$

6. The expanded form of 8,079 is _____.

7. There are 100 ants. If they march in 20 equal rows, how many ants are in each row? _____ ants

8.   58,690
   − 15,489
   _____

For questions 9 and 10, circle the digit in the tens place.

9. 12,506

10. 72,165

Fourth-Grade Math Minutes © 2002 Creative Teaching Press

MINUTE 88

NAME _____

1. 54,818
   − 28,776

2. 63 ÷ 7 =

3. 75 dimes = _____ dollars and _____ nickels

For questions 4 and 5, circle the digit in the thousands place.

4. 59,642

5. 104,265

6. Max bought three cases of soda for $8.00 each. How much did he spend? _____

7. How many minutes and seconds are there in 192 seconds? _____ minutes _____ seconds

8. 451 x 100 =

9. 56 + 24 =

10. The expanded form of 5,020 is _____ .

MINUTE 89

NAME _____

1. $81 \div 9 =$

2. Eighty-seven is an odd number. Circle: True or False

3. $\begin{array}{r} 402 \\ \times\, 311 \\ \hline \end{array}$

4. $\dfrac{57}{8} =$

5. Round 4,658 to the nearest thousand. _____

6. The expanded form of 95,009 is _____.

7. $\dfrac{7}{5} - \dfrac{4}{5} =$

8. $\begin{array}{r} 8{,}658 \\ -\,5{,}497 \\ \hline \end{array}$

For questions 9 and 10, write + or – to make the sentence true.

9. 21×3 _____ $3 = 60$

10. $88 \div 11$ _____ $4 = 12$

MINUTE 90

NAME _____

1. $28 \div 7 =$

2. Gina has a book with 140 pages. If she has read 70 pages of her book, what fraction of the book has she read? _____

3. The most reasonable temperature for a cup of hot cocoa is 40° F.
Circle: True   or   False

4. 16, 24, _____, 40, _____, 56, 64

5.   61,007
     + 91,513

6. $\frac{55}{9} =$

7. The expanded form of 9,073 is _____ .

For questions 8–10, round the number to the nearest hundred.

8. 357 _____

9. 735 _____

10. 537 _____

MINUTE 91

NAME _____

1. Julie planted 120 carrot seeds, 50 lettuce seeds, and 25 tomato seeds. How many seeds did she plant in all? _____ seeds

2. Circle a reasonable measurement for the angle:
   30°   180°   210°

Use <, >, or = to complete questions 3–5.

3. 0.16 _____ 0.4

4. 2.5 _____ 2.05

5. 0.9 _____ 0.90

6. Ben and Milo each want to buy a bike for $135.00 and a helmet for $20.25. How much money do they need altogether? _____

7. Which point is at (3, 1)? _____

8. 49 ÷ 7 =

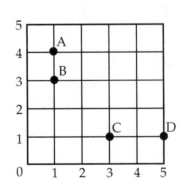

For questions 9 and 10, write how many hours have passed.

9. 6:15 a.m. to 1:15 p.m. = _____

10. 3:00 p.m. to 3:00 a.m. = _____

MINUTE 92

NAME _____

1. _____, _____, _____, 28, 35, 42, 49, 56

2. Circle the figure that is congruent to the shaded figure:

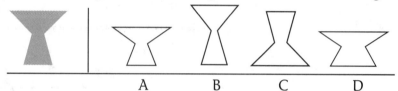

A   B   C   D

In questions 3–5, how would you measure each? Write *cm*, *m*, or *km*.

3. length of your foot _____

4. distance a plane flies across America _____

5. height of your house _____

6. 64 ÷ 8 =

7. 150 – 75 =

For questions 8–10, circle the name of the angle.

8. right   acute   obtuse

9. right   acute   obtuse

10. right   acute   obtuse

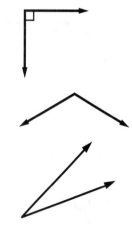

MINUTE 93

NAME _____

1. 51,679
      − 21,201

2. Julie had 50 lettuce plants. Rabbits ate 13 of the plants. How many plants are left? _____ plants

3. What is the volume of the shape? _____

4. Anna bought two sandwiches for $3.00 each and a drink for $1.00. She paid with $15.00. How much change did she receive? _____

For questions 5–7, circle the best measurement for each.

5. length of a pencil   inch   foot   yard

6. temperature for ice-skating   −20°F   28°F   75°F

7. weight of a watermelon   ounce   pound   ton

Use <, >, or = to complete questions 8–10.

8. 6,452 _____ 5,642

9. 1,524 _____ 10,524

10. 6,754 _____ 7,604

MINUTE 94

NAME _____

1. $6.2 + 3.2 =$

2. $\dfrac{49}{6} =$

3. 2 gal = _____ qt

4. Charlotte has a 222 page book. She has read $\dfrac{1}{2}$ of it.
How many pages does she have left to read? _____ pages

5.   15,824
     $+ \ 84,033$

6. $\dfrac{5}{8} + \dfrac{2}{8} =$ _____

7. $48 \div 12 =$ _____

For questions 8–10, write the value of the underlined digit.

8. 7<u>2</u>4.0 = _____

9. 7.<u>2</u>4 = _____

10. 7<u>2</u>.4 = _____

MINUTE 95

NAME _____

1. What is the perimeter of the square? _____

14

2. Henry digs 5 rows to plant 40 seeds. If each row will have the same number of seeds, how many seeds will he plant in each row? _____ seeds

For questions 3 and 4, circle the best measurement for each.

3. height of a tree   inch   foot   mile

4. width of an envelope   inch   foot   yard

5. Nadia earns $2.25 an hour raking leaves. If she rakes leaves for 6 hours, how much money will she earn? _____

6. $84 \div 12 =$ **7.** $17.5 - 2.1 =$

For questions 8–10, write the equivalent fraction.

8. $\dfrac{4}{32} = \dfrac{}{8}$ **9.** $\dfrac{8}{32} = \dfrac{}{4}$

10. $\dfrac{9}{27} = \dfrac{}{3}$

MINUTE 96

NAME _____

1. 42.7 – 12.3 =

2. $\frac{52}{7}$ =

3. The expanded form of 20,641 is _____ .

4. There are 18 children swimming, and 6 are girls. What fraction are girls? _____

5. A _____ is a six-sided polygon.

6. 13 $\overline{)52}$

For questions 7–10, name the solid figure that matches each.

7.  _____

8. _____

9. _____

10. _____

MINUTE 97

NAME _____

1. There are 10 cod, 18 bass, and 10 trout. How many fish are there in all?
    _____ fish

2. 42,215
    + 42,620

3. 2.5 + 6.8 =

4. What is the perimeter of the shape? _____

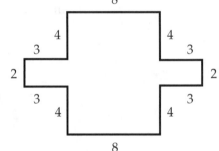

5. 12)‾96‾

6. The expanded form of 7,080 is _____.

For questions 7 and 8, write +, –, or x to make the sentence true.

7. 51 x 10 _____ 10 = 5,100

8. 100 x 70 _____ 10 = 70,000

For questions 9 and 10, circle the digit in the thousands place.

9. 45,624

10. 80,132

MINUTE 98

NAME _____

1. 45 + 55 =

2. 81 ÷ 9 =

3. 40 dimes = _____ dollars

4. _____, _____, _____, 16, 20, 24

5. 240 seconds = _____ minutes

6. 217 x 100 =

7. 12)‾108‾

8. A crab has five pairs of legs. How many legs do two crabs have? _____ legs

Use <, >, or = to complete questions 9 and 10.

9. 2 x 4 _____ 4 + 4

10. 6 + 4 _____ 7 x 2

MINUTE 99

NAME _____

1. There are 150 toys in each case. How many toys are there in 10 cases? _____ toys

2. Fifty-six is an even number.   Circle: True   or   False

3. $12 \overline{)108}$

4. $\dfrac{9}{12} - \dfrac{5}{12} =$

5. A spider has 8 legs. How many legs do 4 spiders have? _____ legs

6. The expanded form of 804,059 is _____.

7. 2, 4, 8, 16, _____, _____, _____, 256

8. Each herd has 40 cows and 2 bulls. How many cows and bulls are there in 4 herds altogether? _____ cows and bulls

For questions 9 and 10, write x or ÷ to make the sentence true.

9. 10 x 80 _____ 10 = 8,000

10. 91 x 1,000 _____ 10 = 9,100

MINUTE 100

NAME _____

1. $81 \div 9 =$

2. $\dfrac{67}{8} =$

3. A quadrilateral has _____ sides and _____ vertices.

4. 18, _____, 36, _____, 54, _____, 72, 81

5. $\dfrac{6}{8} = \dfrac{}{4}$

6. $11\overline{)121}$

7. The expanded form for 504,200 is _____ .

For questions 8–10, round the number to the nearest thousand.

8. 84,375 _____

9. 45,827 _____

10. 62,415 _____

MINUTE ANSWER KEY

MINUTE 1
1. True
2. $7.00
3. 49
4. 35, 5, 7
5. C
6. 3
7. 4
8. 13
9. 5
10. 2

MINUTE 2
1. 7
2. 24, 28, 32
3. 38
4. B
5. 28
6. 42, 6, 7
7. 72
8. yes, ▭
9. yes, ♡
10. no

MINUTE 3
1. 18
2. 27
3. True
4. 40, 5, 8
5. $2.50
6. 42
7. 70
8. <
9. >
10. =

MINUTE 4
1. 83
2. 35
3. 50
4. 36, 36, 4, 9
5. 7
6. 69
7. 112
8. $1/2$
9. $1/3$
10. $1/5$

MINUTE 5
1. False
2. 15
3. 63
4. $4.50
5. 27
6. 9
7. 80
8. 108
9. 5
10. 7

MINUTE 6
1. 95
2. 120
3. True
4. 7
5. 4
6. 12
7. 52
8. 10
9. watermelon
10. pears, oranges

MINUTE 7
1. $1/3$
2. 22
3. 58
4. 12
5. 9
6. 3,000 + 20 + 4
7. 68
8. 4
9. 8
10. 4

MINUTE 8
1. True
2. 50
3. 5
4. 37
5. 171
6. 25¢
7. 81
8. 60
9. 7,800
10. 9

MINUTE 9
1. True
2. 11
3. True
4. 39
5. 4, 4
6. 51
7. 66
8. 3
9. +
10. −

MINUTE 10
1. 104
2. 89
3. 6
4. 5
5. 50
6. 6
7. 6
8. 160
9. 80
10. 50

MINUTE 11
1. 4
2. 90°
3. $28.75
4. 51
5. 45
6. 854
7. 4
8. 15
9. 10
10. 45

MINUTE 12
1. 8
2. 30, 36
3. 72
4. B
5. 36
6. 15
7. 1,024
8. yes, ⬭
9. no
10. no

MINUTE 13
1. 4, 6
2. 9
3. True
4. 34
5. $1.75
6. 1,824
7. 41
8. =
9. <
10. =

MINUTE 14
1. 48
2. 3,976
3. 100
4. 50
5. 6
6. 2
7. 6
8. <
9. >
10. >

MINUTE 15
1. False
2. 1,708
3. 94
4. $3.00
5. 22
6. 84
7. 6
8. $2/3$
9. $3/4$
10. $1/2$

MINUTE 16
1. 140
2. 6
3. 83
4. 4
5. 6, 6
6. 76
7. 2,580
8. drive/carpool
9. skating
10. drive/carpool, skate

MINUTE 17
1. 3,522
2. 30
3. 101
4. 10
5. 7
6. 4,000 + 800 + 50 + 7
7. 56
8. 11
9. 8
10. 9

MINUTE 18
1. 7
2. 93
3. $1.05
4. 60
5. 60¢
6. 6,200
7. 3,090
8. 120
9. 79
10. 3

MINUTE 19
1. $3/8$
2. True
3. 92
4. 9
5. 12
6. 400 + 60 + 5
7. 4,494
8. 76
9. +
10. x

MINUTE 20
1. 85
2. 8
3. 15
4. 5
5. 894
6. 3
7. 2,124
8. 600
9. 500
10. 600

Fourth-Grade Math Minutes © 2002 Creative Teaching Press

MINUTE ANSWER KEY

MINUTE 21
1. 19 pencils
2. 45°
3. 282
4. kilometers
5. centimeters
6. meters
7. 4,326
8. 19
9. 1, 25
10. 1, 15

MINUTE 22
1. 617
2. 21
3. 671
4. A
5. 6 R2
6. 48, 56, 64
7. 4,336
8. acute
9. right
10. obtuse

MINUTE 23
1. 6 R3
2. 483
3. 24
4. 890
5. $2.75
6. 8
7. 2,823
8. >
9. <
10. =

MINUTE 24
1. 4
2. 763
3. 5 R2
4. 6
5. 20
6. 723
7. 4,368
8. 0.6
9. 5 hundreds or 500
10. 7 ones or 7

MINUTE 25
1. 15
2. 14
3. 6 R2
4. 1,039
5. 0.8
6. 754
7. 5,274
8. $\frac{1}{2}$
9. $\frac{1}{5}$
10. $\frac{3}{4}$

MINUTE 26
1. 915
2. 16
3. PNL
4. PNO
5. 7, 7
6. 9 R4
7. 2,484
8. Room 14
9. 60
10. Room 16

MINUTE 27
1. $\frac{4}{10}$ or $\frac{2}{5}$
2. 8
3. 282
4. 15
5. 7 R4
6. 500 + 4
7. 531
8. 2,048
9. 7
10. 4

MINUTE 28
1. 3
2. 782
3. 20
4. 787
5. 54,700
6. 80¢
7. 3,924
8. 90
9. 59
10. 8 R4

MINUTE 29
1. 500
2. True
3. 780
4. 650
5. 5 R3
6. 800 + 40 + 5
7. 1,624
8. 24
9. −
10. +

MINUTE 30
1. 24
2. 928
3. 7 R6
4. 18, 24
5. 761
6. 7
7. 4,149
8. 840
9. 920
10. 1,330

MINUTE 31
1. 35,854
2. 180°
3. $55.50
4. 24
5. 5,509
6. 0.6
7. 786
8. 24
9. 2
10. 3

MINUTE 32
1. 35
2. 8,121
3. 23
4. C
5. 40, 50, 60
6. 689
7. 10,224
8. ray
9. arc
10. plane

MINUTE 33
1. 5
2. 742
3. 120
4. obtuse
5. acute
6. $3.00
7. 45
8. <
9. <
10. >

MINUTE 34
1. 0.4
2. 856
3. 14
4. 8
5. 10,010
6. 15
7. 59,976
8. 42
9. 1 tenth
10. 2 ones

MINUTE 35
1. 20
2. 52
3. cm
4. $10.50
5. 3,644
6. 6
7. 90°
8. $\frac{1}{2}$
9. $\frac{1}{4}$
10. $\frac{1}{3}$

MINUTE 36
1. $\frac{1}{4}$
2. 26,180
3. 6,290
4. 63
5. 8, 8
6. 12
7. obtuse
8. 40
9. Room 10 and Room 14
10. 2

MINUTE 37
1. $\frac{1}{5}$
2. 27
3. 6,516
4. 9
5. 34,722
6. 90,000 + 2,000 + 100 + 50 + 7
7. 778
8. 84
9. 4
10. 8

MINUTE 38
1. 7
2. 98
3. 3
4. A
5. $\overline{AC}$, $\overline{AD}$
6. $\overline{BD}$
7. $3.35
8. 180
9. 920
10. 56

MINUTE 39
1. 6
2. False
3. 0.6
4. 788
5. 12,720
6. 2,000 + 800 + 4
7. 46,494
8. 452
9. x
10. −

MINUTE 40
1. 35
2. 808
3. 5, 5
4. 24
5. 16,630
6. 8
7. 44,124
8. 100
9. 800
10. 900

MINUTE ANSWER KEY

MINUTE 41
1. 12
2. 30°
3. $48.75
4. 2
5. 14,797
6. 2,040
7. 2,461
8. 10
9. 2, 10
10. 3, 30

MINUTE 42
1. 9
2. 16,957
3. 41
4. B
5. 21, 24, 27
6. 2,884
7. 8,760
8. yes,
9. no
10. yes, ‑‑(‑‑‑‑

MINUTE 43
1. 7
2. 7,880
3. 40
4. 13,990
5. $14.00
6. $^5/_8$
7. 4
8. <
9. >
10. <

MINUTE 44
1. 3
2. 2,902
3. 14,529
4. 2
5. 100
6. 0.6
7. 8,636
8. =
9. <
10. <

MINUTE 45
1. 54
2. 6
3. 6,808
4. 60¢
5. 11,094
6. 3,638
7. 100
8. $^2/_3$
9. $^1/_2$
10. $^1/_3$

MINUTE 46
1. 4
2. 3,108
3. 7,927
4. 11,589
5. 5, 5
6. 6
7. 40
8. Tues., Thurs.
9. Sat.
10. Sun.

MINUTE 47
1. $^2/_6$ or $^1/_3$
2. 8
3. 7,909
4. 13
5. 11,883
6. 6,000 + 500 + 40 + 3
7. 8,352
8. 8
9. 4
10. 6

MINUTE 48
1. 2,120
2. 7
3. 10
4. 89
5. 8,219
6. Brand A
7. 2,004
8. 240
9. 8,240
10. 3

MINUTE 49
1. 84
2. False
3. 74
4. 4
5. 15,382
6. 2,000 + 80 + 5
7. 3,081
8. 10,914
9. –
10. +

MINUTE 50
1. 5
2. 7,692
3. 12,299
4. 3
5. 28, 49
6. 7,176
7. 2
8. 2,000
9. 2,000
10. 4,000

MINUTE 51
1. 7
2. 120°
3. 12
4. $177.00
5. 17,258
6. 3,024
7. 2,106
8. B
9. 7
10. 5

MINUTE 52
1. 8
2. 7
3. 23
4. D
5. False
6. 35, 40, 45
7. 4,212
8. line segment
9. edge
10. point

MINUTE 53
1. 15
2. $^4/_{10}$ or $^2/_5$
3. 96
4. 16,966
5. $3.00
6. 22,225
7. 6,921
8. >
9. =
10. <

MINUTE 54
1. 16
2. 6,930
3. 15
4. 3
5. 9,263
6. 3.5
7. True
8. $^2/_3$
9. 3 tenths
10. 5 hundredths

MINUTE 55
1. 300
2. 47,544
3. 20
4. L
5. $\overline{OM}$
6. $\overline{LP}$, $\overline{LN}$, $\overline{LM}$
7. 21
8. 2
9. 3
10. 2

MINUTE 56
1. 9
2. False
3. 5
4. False
5. 6, 6
6. 22,230
7. 1.7
8. Ivy and Max
9. 3
10. Zoe

MINUTE 57
1. 64
2. True
3. $^1/_3$
4. 22
5. 13,132
6. 8,000 + 400 + 2
7. 0.6
8. 0.02
9. 4
10. 9

MINUTE 58
1. 6
2. 6
3. 75¢
4. $^5/_{10}$
5. $^6/_{100}$
6. $^9/_{10}$
7. 59
8. 2
9. 13
10. 90,500

MINUTE 59
1. $^5/_{15}$ or $^1/_3$
2. True
3. 3.7
4. 12,624
5. 50,000 + 4,000 +
   800 + 20 + 2
6. 0.08
7. 0.75
8. 10
9. –
10. +

MINUTE 60
1. 95
2. 5
3. 0.2
4. 1.08
5. 5.6
6. 36, 81
7. 17
8. 800
9. 700
10. 500

Fourth Grade Math Minutes © 2002 Creative Teaching Press

MINUTE ANSWER KEY

MINUTE 61
1. 16
2. 90°
3. $90.50
4. 17
5. 1 in.
6. 4 mi
7. 10 ft
8. A
9. 9
10. 10

MINUTE 62
1. 11
2. 49, 56, 63
3. 49,335
4. D
5. foot
6. mile
7. 12
8. scalene
9. isosceles
10. scalene

MINUTE 63
1. 40
2. 7,488
3. 120
4. $8.85
5. 10
6. False
7. 50,000 + 6,000 + 400 + 90 + 2
8. >
9. >
10. <

MINUTE 64
1. 14
2. 9
3. 7,560
4. 7
5. True
6. $^3/_4$
7. True
8. 7.9
9. 5 tenths
10. 4 hundredths

MINUTE 65
1. 192
2. $^6/_{30}$ or $^1/_5$
3. True
4. $2.25
5. 98,743
6. 18
7. M
8. 4
9. 4
10. 6

MINUTE 66
1. 27
2. =
3. >
4. 3.7
5. True
6. 11
7. False
8. May
9. Apr. and Dec.
10. January to June

MINUTE 67
1. $^6/_9$ or $^2/_3$
2. 105,600
3. 11,556
4. 41
5. 18
6. 40,000 + 50 + 4
7. True
8. 9
9. 4
10. 6

MINUTE 68
1. 8
2. 89
3. $2.40
4. 2
5. 8,052
6. 3¢
7. $\overline{BC}$
8. BCE, BDC
9. 725,000
10. 12

MINUTE 69
1. 44
2. True
3. 20
4. 20,000 + 800 + 50
5. 2.2
6. 0.42
7. 3.01
8. $^5/_8$
9. x
10. x

MINUTE 70
1. 5
2. 2
3. nine and one tenth
4. 30, 42
5. perimeter
6. 17
7. 5,056
8. 43,000
9. 34,000
10. 44,000

MINUTE 71
1. 7.4
2. 210°
3. 247,030
4. $37.00
5. 4 g
6. 12
7. 3
8. B
9. milliliter
10. liter

MINUTE 72
1. 20
2. 63, 72, 81
3. 4,794
4. A
5. milliliters
6. liters
7. 24
8. yes,
9. yes,
10. yes,

MINUTE 73
1. 84°F
2. 62°F
3. 3,000
4. 104,503
5. $3.75
6. 80,000 + 9,000 + 20 + 5
7. 150
8. =
9. >
10. >

MINUTE 74
1. 9.3
2. 15
3. 0.24
4. 2.3
5. 1.09
6. 2
7. 452
8. <
9. <
10. <

MINUTE 75
1. 196
2. 12
3. False
4. $14.00
5. 37°C
6. 94°C
7. 124
8. 3
9. 2
10. 2

MINUTE 76
1. 7
2. $^2/_5$
3. 5.3
4. 5
5. square
6. 5.25, 5.3, 5.32
7. 0.02, 0.2, 2.02
8. Jan.
9. increase
10. May

MINUTE 77
1. 36
2. $^1/_3$
3. True
4. 18
5. 82,038
6. 4,000 + 600 + 2
7. 9:05 p.m.
8. 3:35 p.m.
9. 7
10. 6

MINUTE 78
1. 40,000 + 5,000 + 20 + 9
2. 50
3. $3.50
4. 3.2, 2.5, 1.8
5. 11.52, 10.4, 1.5
6. 12¢
7. 4
8. 65,000
9. 2,808
10. $^7/_8$

MINUTE 79
1. $^3/_6$ or $^1/_2$
2. False
3. 8.9
4. $^3/_4$
5. 1.2
6. 70,000 + 800 + 4
7. 70
8. 120, 125, 130
9. +
10. +

MINUTE 80
1. 6
2. $8^5/_6$
3. 6.3
4. 42, 56
5. 60
6. 232
7. 24
8. 350
9. 480
10. 460

MINUTE ANSWER KEY

MINUTE 81
1. 30°
2. $12.75
3. quart
4. cup
5. gallon
6. B
7. 5,448
8. 15°F
9. 82°F
10. 65°F

MINUTE 82
1. False
2. 6, 12, 18
3. 76,875
4. B
5. 10.7
6. $5\frac{5}{8}$
7. 20,006
8. line segment
9. radius
10. endpoint

MINUTE 83
1. True
2. $5.00
3. 24
4. 2.4
5. 82,802
6. 25,101
7. $5\frac{5}{8}$
8. <
9. >
10. <

MINUTE 84
1. $3\frac{1}{4}$
2. 1.2
3. 18
4. 9
5. False
6. mile
7. ton
8. $\frac{7}{9}$
9. 9 tenths
10. 9 tens

MINUTE 85
1. 128
2. 17,745
3. $20.00
4. 25.6
5. 134,632
6. $6\frac{1}{3}$
7. 500,000 + 10,000 + 2,000 + 7
8. 1
9. 1
10. 1

MINUTE 86
1. 9,521
2. 5.81
3. 156,870
4. $7\frac{2}{5}$
5. $\frac{7}{8}$
6. kg
7. g
8. Sun.
9. Sat.
10. decrease

MINUTE 87
1. $\frac{4}{8}$ or $\frac{1}{2}$
2. L
3. mL
4. 17.5
5. $\frac{5}{6}$
6. 8,000 + 70 + 9
7. 5
8. 43,201
9. 0
10. 6

MINUTE 88
1. 26,042
2. 9
3. 7, 10
4. 9
5. 4
6. $24.00
7. 3, 12
8. 45,100
9. 80
10. 5,000 + 20

MINUTE 89
1. 9
2. True
3. 125,022
4. $7\frac{1}{8}$
5. 5,000
6. 90,000 + 5,000 + 9
7. $\frac{3}{5}$
8. 3,161
9. –
10. +

MINUTE 90
1. 4
2. $\frac{1}{2}$
3. False
4. 32, 48
5. 152,520
6. $6\frac{1}{9}$
7. 9,000 + 70 + 3
8. 400
9. 700
10. 500

MINUTE 91
1. 195
2. 180°
3. <
4. >
5. =
6. $310.50
7. C
8. 7
9. 7
10. 12

MINUTE 92
1. 7, 14, 21
2. C
3. cm
4. km
5. m
6. 8
7. 75
8. right
9. obtuse
10. acute

MINUTE 93
1. 30,478
2. 37
3. 120
4. $8.00
5. inch
6. 28°F
7. pound
8. >
9. <
10. <

MINUTE 94
1. 9.4
2. $8\frac{1}{6}$
3. 8
4. 111
5. 99,857
6. $\frac{7}{8}$
7. 4
8. 2 tens
9. 2 tenths
10. 2 ones

MINUTE 95
1. 56
2. 8
3. foot
4. inch
5. $13.50
6. 7
7. 15.4
8. 1
9. 1
10. 1

MINUTE 96
1. 30.4
2. $7\frac{3}{7}$
3. 20,000 + 600 + 40 + 1
4. $\frac{1}{3}$
5. hexagon
6. 4
7. sphere
8. cube
9. cone
10. cylinder

MINUTE 97
1. 38
2. 84,835
3. 9.3
4. 48
5. 8
6. 7,000 + 80
7. x
8. x
9. 5
10. 0

MINUTE 98
1. 100
2. 9
3. 4
4. 4, 8, 12
5. 4
6. 21,700
7. 9
8. 20
9. =
10. <

MINUTE 99
1. 1,500
2. True
3. 9
4. $\frac{4}{12}$ or $\frac{1}{3}$
5. 32
6. 800,000 + 4,000 + 50 + 9
7. 32, 64, 128
8. 168
9. x
10. ÷

MINUTE 100
1. 9
2. $8\frac{3}{8}$
3. 4, 4
4. 27, 45, 63
5. 3
6. 11
7. 500,000 + 4,000 + 200
8. 84,000
9. 46,000
10. 62,000

Fourth-Grade Math Minutes © 2002 Creative Teaching Press